The Freedom to Fight

By: Anthony Troy Guillory

A Book About Having Dog Fighting and Cockfighting Legal and Regulated.

The Freedom to Fight
Published by Anthony Troy Guillory

For more information:
Anthony Troy Guillory
P.O. Box 176
Branch, LA. 70516

Table of Contents

Chapters:

Introduction

The purpose of this document is to inform and enlighten readers on the "hot topic" of Dog Fighting, with some information on the similar sport of Cock Fighting. Please read this introduction to gather an understanding of what I, the author, am trying to portray. As a lover of animals, an owner of pets and as an experienced spectator of such sports, let it be known I do not consent to the inhumane forms of dog fighting going on in the United States today.

The history of dog/cock fighting is a lengthy one, having documentation dating back to the early Roman Empire at the Coliseum[1]. It was a beloved sport, and was a large source of entertainment. Dog/cock fighting remained popular all over the world for many years.

Now, dog fighting (in the United States specifically) has become illegal. In 48 states you can be charged with a felony if you fight your dogs. Perhaps the law fits the crime, as many who choose to fight their animals are abusing them in the process. Cock fighting has become illegal in 49 states, but it won't be long before Louisiana jumps on the bandwagon.

You may think that fighting your dogs is in fact, abuse. This statement is hardly true, especially when dealing with a passionate owner. It is those like Michael Vick, who has been recently charged with dog fighting and animal abuse that give a sour taste to a great sport.

---

[1] History of dog fighting can be found at   www.wikipedia.org/wiki/dogfighting

4

If you're a parent, you may have your children enrolled in sports. These may be full contact sports in which your children can become injured; yet you let them play. We do this because it gives them exercise, releases stress, anger and gives them a great feeling of self worth. Animals are not so different. Some are meant to be lap dogs, lounging around and barking at the cars going by, much like a child who chooses to be a bookworm, and not a basketball star. Then there are other dogs that love to fight. It is their nature, their instinct and it is our duty to help them fulfill their needs during their short time on earth. Just as we allow our children to show their talents, we should allow dogs to do the same. Of course, strict rules must apply, just as any sport would have.

So please, continue to read this document and absorb all of the information it has to offer. There is a right way to fight dogs, and then there is a wrong way, a terrible way. Unfortunately, it's the wrong way that has been going on for too long, and given the sport a bad reputation, but most importantly, has caused many dogs that loved to fight, to die at the hands of a cold-hearted owner.

Thank you.

A. Troy Guillory

Chapter 1
Rules

Dog fighting/Cock fighting can be done successfully, should strict rules be put into play. This chapter's purpose is to show you an overview of rules that could aid in the legalization of dog fighting.

First, and most importantly: **The purpose of dog fighting/cock fighting MUST NOT be to fight the animals to cause DEATH.** That is an inhumane action on the owner's part. This sort of treatment to the animals is the reason this sport is considered a felony in so many states. When our child is in a wrestling match, we want him to pin his enemy and claim his title as champion. We would never dream of letting the ones we love fight to the death, or let them go untreated should they get injured. Why would we let another creature suffer?

Registration: All cock fighters and dog fighters MUST be licensed by the state. Each person who owns, breeds, or fights these animals must pay a sum of money per year to own, breed or fight either dogs or gamecocks. If said person has both dogs and gamecocks to fight, the sum paid for registration should be doubled. An example would be $200 to register your dog. It would be $400 to register multiple dogs.

Each puppy that is born must be registered through the state upon birth. Litter registration is possible, but each puppy must be accounted for. When it comes time for the rolling[2] to begin, all rolls must be performed in an approved arena or "pit" with full paying members

---

[2] Rolling is a slang term, popular in dog/cock fighting. It is simply another term for "fighting."

allowed to witness these rolls. If it is determined that the dog should be culled[3], and then it is to be humanely euthanized by a licensed and state approved veterinarian and documented accordingly.

If the owner decides that euthanasia is not the right choice for the dog, and can provide care to the animal until is recovers fully, it should be done. The dog should also be spayed/neutered to prevent the dog from breeding. This could cause undesirable traits to pass along to the dog's offspring, should he ever mate. This would allow the breeding of only the best dogs. It would also help to stop the over population of dogs with undesirable traits, like over-aggressiveness. Less dogs running around with anger management issues means less chances they will break free from their yards to attack innocent people and other animals.

Drugs: The use or sale of illegal drugs during fights or in the home of an owner who fights his animals will NOT be tolerated. Should the owner get busted for drugs, or if drugs are found where animals are kept, then all dogs or gamecocks will be taken away from the owner. If necessary, these animals will be euthanized to keep them from entering the wrong hands. This is called a "Zero Tolerance" law.

Also, if you have a criminal record, you will not be allowed to own or breed animals for fighting. This does not include moving violations or other civil crimes that remain on your record for a bit once you've paid. This does include things like domestic assault, theft of any degree and fraud. All felonies no matter what nature will result in the

---

[3] Culled: to exterminate.

person being banned. No exceptions to the rule, no matter how established they are in the sport.

For gamecock fights, I don't remember there actually being a name given to the rules, but for "gaff" fights there are the Wortham Rules. In my state of Louisiana, cock fighting is still legal, so I have raised and fought natural heel fighters and the rules were:

Pit size is to be 16'x16'

Each corner has only a medium sized stainless steel bowl with fresh water for use during pittings.

Only the judge and a handler for each cock as well as the cocks are allowed in the pit at one time.

Both cocks are brought to the center and allowed to peck at each other to show aggression. This is however, not necessary.

Each cock is then brought to its respective corner and when the judge has given the word, the cocks are released and the fight begins.

The roosters are allowed to fight and the only time the handlers are allowed to touch the birds is with the judges' permission.

The judge orders the birds to be picked up and given 20 seconds to handle the bird in their corner. On the count of 20, the roosters are again released.

The birds are given a 10 second count to fight and if they don't "scratch" to each other from each corner, then they are to be picked up and given another 20 second pitting. Then the birds are brought to the "scratch line" or "short line," which is 2 feet away from each other, and released.

If no bird attempts to fight by throwing the beak in a pecking fashion or by trying to fight with its legs on 3 consecutive 10-second counts then the match is considered a draw, having no winner or loser.

If only one attempts to fight, then that one is considered the winner after 3 consecutive 10-second counts after he last threw his beak.

If both are throwing the beak then the short line, work continues until only one cock throws the beak and is declared the winner.

If at any time a cock is "hack" and not game, the fight is over. This would mean if the bird were running around screaming.

No bird is allowed to be in a fight pit when it does not want to be in the pit. This is important and should be noted in any case where animals are fighting.

Many use Cuban rules for cock fighting. Here are those rules:

Pit size is the same, but no handlers are allowed in the pit.

Each fight can last for only 20 minutes. No handlers or pitters allowed in the pit, only the judge and the birds.

If no bird is declared the winner in a 20-minute time limit, then the fight is a draw and both birds are picked up and brought home to be taken care of, and to fight another day.

I agree with the above rules but don't see how we would be breeding "GAMECOCKS," but instead are breeding cocks that hopefully kill within the 20 minutes, and the gameness of the birds are being bred out of the bloodline.

I think we should have the best of both, where after 20 minutes if no bird is declared the winner, then the birds are brought to a drag pit and allowed to continue fighting until 1 or both stop fighting.

Gamecock Boxing is another option.

Each bird is fitted with leather boxing gloves (yes, boxing gloves) and every cock fighter uses boxing gloves to spar his gamecocks.

The birds are allowed to box each other until one quits. The last one standing is declared the winner, and the loser needs only to heal his bruises, and possibly his ego.

The above regulations and standards are the most humane ways to keep this sport legal. We must adhere to these rules to ensure that the sport is fair, safe and that the people participating are doing it for the right reasons.

Chapter 2
Humane?

Some of you may be confused with what the Humane Society of the United States really stands for. It has very little to do with your local animal shelters. They may use the name Humane Society in print, but it goes very little past that.

The purpose of the Humane Society is not to fund small animal shelters and help keep strays of the street. Their true purpose is to accumulate millions of dollars each year for themselves, while targeting people like cattle farmers, trying to put them out of business. They also want to put a stop to circus acts using animals, and close down zoos. This may sound ridiculous to some, as many zoos are responsible, and help breed animals that are close to extinction.

Many involved with the Humane Society also feel that it is cruel to consume meat, dairy and egg products. They'd like to see the United States full of caring vegetarians. Hunting is also against the morals of the Humane Society. They would rather let you hit a deer with your car on the interstate, than allow hunting to control an overpopulated area.

But don't let this sugar coating of kindness fool you. The Humane Society affiliated shelters do euthanize animals, just in smaller numbers than shelters who don't associate themselves with the HSUS. Obviously, if an animal is sick, or severely injured, they will put them down. When it comes to over-populated shelters, the "no-kill" shelters DO kill. They usually send the animals to another clinic to be euthanized. They also donate them to local veterinary colleges, where med student practice operations on these animals. The animals are immediately put down, tossed into a collection bin, and taken to the crematorium. However, the best excuse a no-kill establishment affiliated with the HSUS is claiming the animal to be "inadaptable." This means the cat is too "feral"; the dog is to "angry" or whichever term they chose. So instead of trying to condition these animals to be better pets, they simply kill them off.

When it comes to dog fighting, or any animal fighting, the Humane Society is obviously against it.[4] They claim that dog fighting leads to dogs attacking children. This is a preposterous statement. Just because a dog is fighting, doing what he loves to do, doesn't mean he will just take off and seek a child to bite. Dogs who attack are untrained animals that need discipline. Those who *properly* train their dogs for fighting, and general well being, will not have a ticking time bomb for an animal. Dogs are smart creatures. They understand when a fight is a fight, and when to obey their masters. The Humane Society also states that dogs can confuse children to be a small animal. Once again, what evidence do they have to back these accusations? None.

Their concerns about dog fighting continue to include children. Often times, children have been spectators at these events, according to the HSUS. They say allowing a child to watch a dogfight desensitizes them, making them less compassionate towards animals. I suppose you shouldn't bring your child to a hockey game either, because they will be

---

[4] Find more information about the United States Humane Society by visiting their official website at www.hsus.org.

insensitive to human beings as well. It is the duty of the parent to teach the child to be a lover of animals, and respect the sport of dog fighting. A child can easily understand that when dogs fight, it's OK because that is what they are trained to do. The child can also understand that this doesn't mean he can be cruel to animals. It's a simple right and wrong lecture every parent tells his or her child. "Just because you see BLANK doesn't mean that you should run out and do BLANK." It's similar to the conversations a parent may have with a child in regards to violence on television.

So in conclusion to the not-so-Humane Society, remember: they are hardly saints. They could care less about under funding in shelters, stray animals, animal control, and euthanasia to shelter animals. They are more concerned with getting big and rich and exploiting simple dairy farmers. In the section of their website that targets dog fighting, they barely speak about the dogs themselves. They're more concerned with illegal gambling, and large amounts of money being exchanged during fights. Of course, this is an issue, but perhaps the HSUS could step in and help regulate what they don't approve of within the sport, inside of zoos and circus acts. This would prove them more helpful then just trying to eliminate all of these great American pastimes.

Chapter 3
Giving the Sport a Bad Name:
The Michael Vick Case

Atlanta Falcons quarterback Michael Vick has recently been tried
for illegal dog fighting. In the summer of 2007, he was arrested for
several felony counts of dog fighting and illegal gambling. In August of
2007, he entered a plea bargain, bringing the charges down to one felony.
He was found guilty for *conspiracy of dog fighting* and will serve 23
months in prison. The gambling charges were dropped. He was involved
with a dog-fighting group called "The Bad Newz Kennels."

So how have Michael Vick's actions hurt legitimate dog fighting?
There are so many ways. Let's take a look at how this "dog fighter" has
forced those who want to legalize dog fighting to hold their breath. His
actions have caused many to take a few steps back on the road to progress.

First, take a look at the conditions the dogs were kept in. 49 dogs
were confiscated from Vick's acreage in Virginia. The dogs were not
properly taken care of, living in filth without adequate food. This was
most likely part of Vick's plan to make them "angry." You don't get a
champion fighter by cramming them into small cages and starving them.

Vick also took it upon himself to euthanize animals when he didn't
favor them. If he would get a new dog to fight, and the dog wasn't much
of a fighter during testing rounds, Vick would hang or drown them
personally. Not all dogs wish to be fighters. Who is he to decide if that
dog should live or die? Legal fighting would mean that only licensed

veterinarians could euthanize an animal. Also, not wanting to be a fighter is not grounds for termination of a dog. There is no room for animal cruelty in legitimate dog fighting.

Yet cruelty was the only thing going on at Michael Vick's underground dog fighting ring. Dogs would fight, and the wounded would be killed, or left to die. There are no records of Vick being concerned for his animals or providing treatment. There are however, reports of finding dogs wounded, untreated and lying on blood soaked carpeting when police searched Vick's multi-million dollar home.

There is hope for these animals. One sadly was court ordered to be euthanized, due to untamable aggression, but the other dogs can be rehabilitated. They can move on from the horror that Vick put them through, and find a loving home. If after all they've been through, those dogs still wish to fight; there should be a way for them to do something they love. When you legalize dog fighting and set guidelines, you can provide a positive atmosphere and experience both dog and owner will appreciate. If we continue to keep dog fighting illegal and underground, it will continue to be run by drug lords, gangs and general lowlife. These people have no respect for the law or the lives of others, especially that of animals. These rings serve a purpose only of animal cruelty and illegal activities. These dogs are treated like garbage…or worse.

Those who continue to abuse the sport of dog fighting must be punished. It is not a silly game, or a thoroughfare to sell illegal drugs. It is a sport. A sport that many take seriously, and it is those same people who need to help set rules and educate others.

Chapter 4
The History of the Breed

It is a fact that those who dog fight in the United States will fight pit bulls the most out of any breed of dog. This has caused many to believe that this particular sort of dog is nothing but a ticking time bomb. Many places in the United States are forcing owners of pit bulls to abandon their dogs. Some states do not have a Grandfather's clause to keep those who already own the animal, safe; they must get rid of their animals. We're going to look at the history of the pit bull, as well as some other "dangerous" and docile breeds to note why the pit bull is so successful in the ring, but also possibly not as big of a threat as society is making them out to be.

Pit bulls originated in England as a breed containing a member of the terrier family and the bulldog. Bulldogs are known for their strong, muscular bodies and stature, and the terrier is famous for taking down small animals that would destroy crops. It is a marriage of two great breeds to create a valuable animal. You can see how their best assets made them prime animals for dog fighting.

Now let it be mentioned that a "pit bull" can be quite a combination of different dogs. Let's look at wikipedia.com to get a better understanding of how to define a pit bull:

A term commonly used to describe several types of dogs with similar physical characteristics. Its use in media is often vague and rarely descriptive of specific breeds. There are several physically similar breeds that are often termed "pit bull", including the American Pit Bull Terrier, American Staffordshire Terrier, the Staffordshire Bull Terrier, the Bull Terrier, the Perro de Presa Canario, Cane Corso, and Argentine Dogos. These breeds are usually not included by name in any Breed Specific Legislation, but are sometimes included because of a broad definition as to what a pit bull actually is. All of these breeds as well as many others (including Great Danes, Newfoundlands and Rottweilers) are members of breed.[5]

So we can see from the statement above that many dogs are classified in the "pit bull" range. So when the media comes out with reports stating that "half of the dog bites reported in the United States were caused by a pit bull," we can recognize that this is not just one specific dog. There are many combinations of dogs that can be deemed a pit bull, and with so many types, it could seem more realistic. If a large percentage of the attacks were from a shi-tzu, we might find that hard to believe, as that would be a high attack rate for one animal. We now understand (if you didn't already) that pit bulls can stand for many types of dogs, where as a shi-tzu is simply...a shi-tzu.

Now, let's take a look at some of the myths surrounding the pit bull. This will help bring understanding and truth to the animal, which has gathered quite a bad rap around the United States.

MYTH: All Pit Bulls are mean and vicious.

---

[5] For more information on the history of the pit bull please check out
http://en.wikipedia.org/wiki/Pit_bull#History

It is reported on temperament tests conducted by the American Temperament Test Society that Pit Bulls had a passing rate of 82% or better -- compared to only 77% of the general dog population.

MYTH: A Pit Bull that shows aggression towards an animal will go for people next.

Many working breeds have antipathy towards other animals - coonhounds go mad at the sight of a raccoon, foxhounds will not hesitate to tear a dog-like fox to shreds and greyhounds live to chase and maul rabbits and even dog-like coyotes. Even the ever-friendly beagle will slaughter a rabbit, given the chance.

And yet the greyhound, coon and foxhound and beagle are among the friendliest of breeds towards humans. And it is the same with the pit bulldog. His work through the years has been control of other animals - never humans. A correct pit bull is more often than not submissive toward all humans, and adores children.

MYTH: Pit Bulls brains swell/never stop growing.

This rumor started with the Doberman, and has since been said about game-bred dogs in general. The concept of an animal's brain swelling or growing too large and somehow causing the animal to "go crazy" is not based in truth in any way. If it were the case, the animal would die once he outgrew his skull.[6]

Since we have cleared up a few of the popular misconceptions surrounding pit bulls, let's take a look how some cities in the United States feel about the breed. It's saddening to know that even after hard proof in the pit bull's favor, they are still considered dangerous to many uninformed people. Here are the names of the cities, states, status of the law and punishment for having a pit bull:

Place	Status	Type	Date	Details
Delta, Utah	Active	City	N/A	N/A
Independence, Missouri	Active	City	2006	N/A
Springville, Utah	Active	City	N/A	N/A

---

[6] Find more information online about the myths, facts and general information surrounding pit bulls at www.pitbulllovers.com

Miami-Dade County, Florida	Active	County	1989	Section 5 Code 17: "It is illegal in Miami-Dade County to own any dog which substantially conforms to a pit bull breed dog, unless it was specially registered with Miami-Dade County prior to 1989. Acquisition or keeping of a pit bull dog: $500.00 fine and County Court action to force the removal of the animal from Miami-Dade County."
Council Bluffs, Iowa	Active	City	2004	N/A
Royal City, Washington	Active	City	1/12/2007	N/A
Denver, Colorado	Active	City	5/9/2005	First banned in 1980s, but later revoked
Prince George's	Active	City	1996	N/A

County, Maryland				
Yonkers, NY	Active	City	11/6/2006	N/A
Springfield, Missouri	Active	City	7/13/2005	N/A
Oklahoma	Proposed	State	5/21/2005	N/A
Shelbyville, California	Proposed	City	11/18/2006	N/A
New York City, NY	Proposed	City	12/28/2006	N/A
Aurora, Colorado	Proposed	City	9/27/2005	N/A
Youngstown, Ohio	Proposed	City	1/10/1999	N/A
Richland, Washington	Proposed	City	12/21/2006	N/A
Tupelo, Mississippi	Proposed	City	9/28/2006	N/A
Parker, Colorado	Proposed	City	1/17/2006	N/A

Chicago, Illinois	Proposed	City	11/17/2005	N/A
Enumclaw, Washington	Active	City	N/A	N/A
Garfield Heights, Ohio	Active	City	10/24/2007	60 days in jail and or $1,000 fine if owner does not comply with city law.
Sparta, Tennessee	Active	City	N/A	N/A
Lexington, Kentucky	Active	City	10/28/2006	5 years in jail and or $10,000 fine if owner does not comply with city law.
Melvindale, Michigan	Active	City	4/4/2005	$100.00 fine or 30 days in jail.

7

It's interesting to see how many cities in the United States are up in arms, ready to cast aside a pit bull. Yet we went on a frenzy in the early 1990's because of a Disney cartoon, and bought our children Dalmatians, an extremely neurotic and aggressive animal. These dogs made such bad

---

[7] This chart is located at http://en.wikipedia.org/wiki/Pit_bull

pets, a rescue society had to be formed to take in all the animals that the uneducated buyers couldn't handle. "Save the Dalmatians and kill off the pit bull?" If Disney made a movie about 101 loveable pit bull puppies, everyone would
have run out and bought one of those too, except they'd be a lot happier.

Let's end this chapter on a lighter note. For all of the pit bull lovers out there, this is a top 10 list, courtesy of pitbulllovers.com.

Ten Facts About Pit Bulls Every One Should Know

1. Pit Bulls are commonly used as therapy dogs. Whether they are visiting a senior care facility or helping someone recover from an emotional accident, pit bulls are making a mark as outstanding therapy dogs.

2. Pit Bulls are used in Search and Rescue work.

3. Pit Bulls serve as narcotic and bomb sniffing dogs. One pit bull, Popsicle (named that because he was found in an old freezer) has the largest recorded single drug find in Texas history.

4. Pit Bulls are great with kids. They weren't referred to as the "nanny's dog" for nothing. That's for sure.

5. Pit Bulls are not human aggressive. The American Pit Bull Terrier as a breed is not human aggressive. In fact, quite the opposite is true of the breed. They are gentle and loving dogs. Like any dog individuals can be unsound and have behavior problems.

6. The Pit Bull was so popular in the early 1900's they were our mascot not only in World War One, but World War Two as well. They were featured on recruiting and propaganda posters during this time period.

7. Sgt. Stubby: A pit bull war hero. Stubby was wounded in action twice. He saved his entire platoon by warning them of a poison gas attack and he single handedly captured a German spy.

8. Pete the Pup on the original Little Rascals was a pit bull.

9. Pit Bulls score an 83.4% passing rate with the American Temperament Test Society. That's better than the popular Border collie (a breed who scores 79.6%).

10. They are dogs… not killing machines.

Sadie. This photo cannot be copied or used in any way without the consent of the author.

Chapter 5
Know Your Rights

To say that dog/cock fighting is illegal is a deprivation of our rights as human beings. It is basically unconstitutional. There is a generalized religious belief that animals cannot enter Heaven. This is due to their lack of souls. If you're not religious, then perhaps you can still see some truth to the previous statement. Change out the word *souls* with *reason*. Animals are simply mindless creatures, possessing a minimal amount of intelligence. Their diminutive brains communicate by letting them know when they're hungry, tired and when it's time to mate. Without the ability to reason, they cannot have rights. Humans decide which path is true for our animals to take. That is our right.

Dogs are property, plain and simple. As humans, we are allowed to do with our property as we see fit, so long that is does not bring any dilemma to any other humans. Consider fighting your animals, as you would consider being a homeowner. When your house is no longer inhabitable, old and ready to retire, do you simply drizzle gasoline throughout and light a match? No. There are rules. You would call a contractor and have the house torn down, complying with the rules of demolition. When your dog lacks the aspiration to fight you do not just dispose of them haphazardly. You follow the rules and contact a licensed vet.

However, in the United States, animals were given rights. There is an animal welfare act put in place, which gives these creatures "rights." Not every part of this act is insane; some of it does have merit. For example, we shouldn't cause harm to animals by means of torture. As humans, we are the highest living being on this earth. We should not stoop so low as to cause unnecessary physical harm to another living thing, no matter how insignificant the life is. This Animal Welfare Act of 1976 is public law, and therefore is shown below in the following pages for you to read for yourself.

Public Law 94-279 Animal Welfare Act Amendments of 1976

Public Law 94-279
94th Congress, S. 1941
April 22, 1976

Note: In this version of the amendment, brackets, [], indicate notes found in the corresponding margin of the hardcopy document.

To amend the Act of August 24, 1966, as amended, to increase the protection afforded animals in transit and to assure humane treatment of certain animals, and for other purposes.

[Animal Welfare Act Amendments of 1976. 7 USC 2131 note. 7 USC 2131 note. 7 USC 2131.] Be it enacted by the Senate and House of Representatives of the United States of America in Congress assembled, That this Act may be cited as the "Animal Welfare Act Amendments of 1976".

SEC. 2. Section 1 of the Act of August 24, 1966 (80 Stat. 350, as amended by the Animal Welfare Act of 1970, 84, Stat. 1560; 7 U.S.C. 2131-2155) is amended to read as follows:

"Section 1. (a) This Act may be cited as the `Animal Welfare Act'.

"(b) The Congress finds that animals and activities which are regulated under this Act are either in interstate or foreign commerce or substantially affect such commerce or the free flow thereof, and that regulation of animals and activities as provided in this Act is necessary to prevent and eliminate burdens upon such commerce and to effectively regulate such commerce, in order--

"(1) to insure that animals intended for use in research facilities or for exhibition purposes for use as pets are provided humane care and treatment;

"(2) to assure the humane treatment of animals during transportation in commerce; and

"(3) to protect the owners of animals from the theft of their animals by preventing the sale or use of animals which have been stolen.

The Congress further finds that it is essential to regulate, as provided in this Act, the transportation, purchase, sale, housing, care, handling, and treatment of animals by carriers or by persons or organizations engaged in using them for research or experimental purposes of for exhibition purposes or holding them for sale as pets or for any such purpose or use".

[7 USC 2132.] SEC. 3. Section 2 of such Act is amended--

(1) by striking out subsection © and (d) thereof and inserting lieu thereof the following:

[Definitions.] "© The term `commerce' means trade, traffic, transportation, or other commerce--

"(1) between a place in a State and any place outside of such State, or between points within any territory, possession, or the District of Columbia;

"(2) which affects trade, traffic, transportation, or other commerce described in paragraph (1).

"(d) The term `State' means a State of the United States, the District of Columbia, the Commonwealth of Puerto Rico, the Virgin Islands, Guam, American Samoa, or any other territory of possession of the United States;"

(2) by striking out the term "affecting commerce" in subsections (e) and (f) and inserting in lieu thereof "in commerce";

(3) by revising paragraph (f) thereof to read as follows:

"(f) The term `dealer' means any person who, in commerce, for compensation or profit, delivers for transportation, or transports, except as a carrier, buys, or sells, or negotiates the purchase or sale of, (1) any dog or other animal whether alive or dead for research, teaching, exhibition, or use as a pet, or (2) any dog for hunting, security, or breeding purposes, except that this term does not include--

"(i) a retail pet store except such store which sells any animals to a research facility, an exhibitor, or a dealer; or

"(ii) any person who does not sell, or negotiate the purchase or sale of any wild animal, dog, or cat, and who derives no more than $500 gross income from the sale of other animals during any calendar year;"

(4) by deleting "and" at the end of paragraph (g) and inserting in lieu thereof the following: "With respect to a dog, the term means all dogs including those used for hunting, security, or breeding purposes;" and

(5) by deleting the period at the end of paragraph (h) and inserting a semicolon in lieu thereof.

[7 USC 2132.] SEC. 4. Section 2 of such Act is further amended by adding thereto two new paragraphs to read:

["Intermediate handler."] "(i) The term `intermediate handler' means any person including a department, agency, or instrumentality of the United States or of any State or local government (other than a dealer, research facility, exhibitor, any person excluded from the definition of a dealer, research facility, or exhibitor, an operator of an auction sale, or a carrier) who is engaged in any business in which he receives custody of animals in connection with their transportation in commerce; and

["Carrier."] "(j) The term `carrier' means the operator of any airline, railroad, motor carrier, shipping line, or other enterprise, which is engaged in the business of transporting any animals for hire."

[7 USC 2134, 2141, 2142.] SEC. 5. Sections 4, 11, and 12 of such Act are amended by striking out "affecting commerce" and inserting in lieu thereof "in commerce."

[7 USC 2136.] SEC. 6. Section 6 of such Act is amended by inserting after the term "research facility" a comma and the term "every intermediate handler, every carrier."

[7 USC 2139.] SEC. 7. Section 9 of such Act is amended by inserting after the term "section 12 of this Act," the term "or an intermediate handler, or a carrier" and by deleting the term "or an operator of an auction sale as well as of such person." at the end of section 9 and substituting there for the following term: "operator of an auction sale, intermediate handler, or carrier, as well as of such person."

[7 USC 2140. Record retention.] SEC. 8. Section 10 of such Act is amended by deleting the phrase "upon forms supplied by the Secretary" from the first sentence and by inserting between the second and third sentences thereof the following: "At the request of the Secretary, any regulatory agency of the Federal Government which requires records to be maintained by intermediate handlers and carriers with respect to the transportation, receiving, handling, and delivery of animals on forms prescribed by the agency, shall require there to be included in such forms such information as the Secretary may require for the effective administration of this Act. Such information shall be retained for such reasonable period of time as the Secretary may prescribe. If regulatory agencies of the Federal Government do not prescribe requirements for any such forms, intermediate handlers and carriers shall make and retain for such reasonable period as the Secretary may prescribe such records with respect to the transportation, receiving, handling, and delivery of animals as the Secretary may prescribe."

[7 USC 2143. Standards. Rules and regulations.]] SEC. 9. Section 13 of such Act is amended by designating the provisions thereof as subsection (a) and by adding, after the second sentence therein, new sentences to read: "The Secretary shall also promulgate standards to govern the transportation in commerce, and the handling, care, and treatment in connection therewith, by intermediate handlers, air carriers, of animals consigned or other person, or any department, agency, or instrumentality of the United States or of any State or local government, for transportation in commerce. The Secretary shall have authority to promulgate such rules and regulations as he determines necessary to assure humane treatment of animals in the course of their transportation in commerce including requirements such as those with respect to containers, feed, water, rest, ventilation, temperature, and handling."

[7 USC 2143.] SEC. 10. Section 13 of such Act, as amended, is further amended by adding at the end thereof new subsections (b), ©, and (d) to read:

"(b) No dogs or cats, or additional kinds or classes of animals designated by regulation of the Secretary, shall be delivered by any dealer, research facility, exhibitor, operator of an auction sale, or department, agency, or instrumentality of the United States or of any State or local government, to any intermediate handler or carrier for transportation in commerce, or received by any such handler or carrier for such transportation from any such person, department, agency, or instrumentality, unless the animal is accompanied by a certificate issued by a veterinarian licensed to practice veterinary medicine, certifying that he inspected the animal on a specified date, which shall not be more than ten days before such delivery, and, when so inspected, the animal appeared free of any infectious disease or physical abnormality which would endanger the animal or animals or other animals or endanger public health: Provided, however, That the Secretary may by regulation provide exceptions to this certification requirement, under such conditions as he may prescribe in the regulations, for animals shipped to research facilities for purposes of research, testing or experimentation requiring animals not eligible for such certification. Such certificates received by the intermediate handlers and the carriers shall be retained by them as provided by regulations of the Secretary, in accordance with section 10 of this Act.

[7 USC 2140.] "© No dogs or cats, or additional kinds or classes of animals designated by regulation of the Secretary, shall be delivered by

34

any person to any intermediate handler or carrier for transportation in commerce except to registered research facilities if they are less than such age as the Secretary may by regulation prescribe. The Secretary shall designate additional kinds and classes of animals and may prescribe different ages for particular kinds or classes of dogs, cats, or designated animals, for the purposes of this section, when he determines that such action is necessary or adequate to assure their humane treatment in connection with their transportation in commerce.

"(d) No intermediate handler or carrier involved in the transportation of any animal in commerce shall participate in any arrangement or engage in any practice under which the cost of such animal or the cost of the transportation of such animal is to be paid and collected upon delivery of the animal to the consignee, unless the consignor guarantees in writing the payment of transportation charges for any animal not claimed within a period of 48 hours after notice to the consignee of arrival of the animal, including, where necessary, both the return transportation charges and an amount sufficient to reimburse the carrier for all out-of-pocket expenses incurred for the care, feeding, and storage of such animals."

[7 USC 2145.] SEC. 11. Section 15 of such Act is amended by inserting after the term "exhibition" in the first sentence, a comma and the term "or administration of statutes regulating the transportation in commerce or handling in connection therewith of any animals", and by adding the following at the end of the sentence: "Before promulgating any standard governing the air transportation and handling in connection therewith, of animals, the Secretary shall consult with the Secretary of Transportation who shall have the authority to disapprove any such standard if he notifies the Secretary, within 30 days after such consultation, that changes in its provisions are necessary in the interest of flight safety. The Interstate Commerce Commission, the Civil Aeronautics Board, and the Federal Maritime Commission, to the extent of their respective lawful authorities, shall take such action as is appropriate to implement any standard established by the Secretary with respect to a person subject to regulation by it."

[7 USC 2146.] SEC. 12. (a) Subsection (a) of section 16 of such Act is amended by inserting the term "intermediate handler, carrier," in the first sentence after the term "exhibitor," each time the latter term appears in the sentence; by inserting before the period in the second sentence, a comma and the term "or (5) such animal is held by an intermediate handler or a carrier"; and by deleting the term "or" before the term "(4)" in the second sentence.

(b) Subsection © of section 16 of such Act is amended by striking the words "sections 19(b) and 20(b)" in the last sentence and inserting in lieu thereof the words "section 19©."

[7 USC 2149.] SEC. 13. Section 19 of such Act is amended to read as follows:

[License suspension and revocation. 7 USC 2142. Notice, hearing.] "(a) If the Secretary has reason to believe that any person licensed as a dealer, exhibitor, or operator of an auction sale subject to section 12 of this Act, has violated or is violating any provision of this Act, or any of the rules or regulations or standards promulgated by the Secretary hereunder, he may suspend such person's license temporarily, but not to exceed 21 days, and after notice and opportunity for hearing, may suspend for such additional period as he may specify, or revoke such license, if such violation is determined to have occurred.

[Civil penalty. Notice, hearing. Civil action. Penalty.] "(b) Any dealer, exhibitor, research facility, intermediate handler, carrier, or operator of an auction sale subject to section 12 of this Act, that violates any provision of this Act, or any rule, regulation, or standard promulgated by the Secretary there under, may be assessed a civil penalty by the Secretary of not more than $1,000 for each such violation, and the Secretary may also make an order that such person shall cease and desist from continuing such violation. Each violation and each day during which a violation continues shall be a separate offense. No penalty shall be assessed or cease and desist order issued unless such person is given notice and opportunity for a hearing with a penalty and making a cease and desist order shall be final and conclusive unless the affected person files an appeal from the Secretary's order with the appropriate United States Court of Appeals. The Secretary shall give due consideration to the appropriateness of the penalty with respect to the size of the business of the person involved, the gravity of the violation, the person's good faith, and the history of previous violations. Any such civil penalty may be compromised by the Secretary. Upon any failure to pay the penalty assessed by a final order under this section, the Secretary shall request the Attorney General to institute a civil action in a district court of the United States or other United States court for any district in which such person is found or resides or transact business, to collect the penalty, and such court shall have jurisdiction to hear and decide any such action. Any person who knowingly fails to obey a cease and desist order made by the Secretary under this section shall be subject to a civil penalty of $500 for each offense, and each day during which such failure continues shall be deemed a separate offense.

[Review. 7 USC 2142.] "© Any dealer, exhibitor, research facility, intermediate handler, carrier, or operator of an auction sale subject to section 12 of this Act, aggrieved by a final order of the Secretary issued pursuant to this section may, within 60 days after entry of such an order, seek review of such order in the appropriate United States Court of Appeals in accordance with the provisions of section 2341, 2343 through 2350 of title 28, United States Code, and such court shall have exclusive jurisdiction to enjoin, set aside, suspend (in whole or in part), or to determine the validity of the Secretary's order.

[Penalties.] "(d) Any dealer, exhibitor, or operator of an auction sale subject to section 12 of this Act, who knowingly violates any provision of this Act shall, on conviction thereof, be subject to imprisonment for not more than 1 year, or a fine of not more than $1,000, or both. Prosecution of such violations shall, to the maximum extent practicable, be brought initially before United States magistrates as provided in section 636 of title 28, United States Code, and sections 3401 and 3402 of title 18, United States Code, and, with the consent of the Attorney General, may be conducted, at both trial and upon appeal to district court, by attorneys of the United States Department of Agriculture."

[Repeal. 7 USC 2150.] SEC. 14. Section 20 of such Act is hereby repealed.

[7 USC 2154.Infra. Effective date.] SEC. 15. Section 24 of such Act is amended by inserting the following at the end of the section: "Not withstanding the other provisions of this section, compliance by intermediate handlers, and carriers, and other persons with those provisions of this Act, as amended, with respect to intermediate handlers and carriers, and such regulations shall be promulgated no later that 9 months after the enactment of the Animal Welfare Act Amendments of 1976; and compliance by dealers, exhibitors, operators of auction sales, and research facilities with other provisions of this Act, as so amended, and the regulations there under, shall commence upon the expiration of 90 days after enactment of the Animal Welfare Act Amendments of 1976: Provided, however, That compliance by all persons with paragraphs (b), ©, and (d) of section 13 and with section 26 of this Act, as so amended, shall commence upon the expiration of said ninety-day period. In all other respects, said amendments shall become effective upon the date of enactment."

[7 USC 2155.] SEC. 16. Section 25 of such Act is amended by deleting from subsection (2) the word "and" where it last appears, deleting the period at the end of subsection (3) and inserting "; and" in lieu thereof, and by inserting after subsection (3) the following new subsection:

"(4) recommendations and conclusions concerning the aircraft environment as it relates to the carriage of live animals in air transportation.".

SEC. 17. Such Act is amended by adding at the end thereof the following new section:

[Animal fighting venture, prohibition. 7 USC 2156.] "SEC. 26. (a) It shall be unlawful for any person to knowingly sponsor or exhibit any animal in any animal fighting venture to which any animal was moved in interstate or foreign commerce.

"(b) It shall be unlawful for any person to knowingly sell, buy, transport, or deliver to another person or receive from another person for purposes of transportation, in interstate for foreign commerce, any dog or other animal for purposes of having the dog or other animal participate in an animal fighting venture.

[Penalties.] "© It shall be unlawful for any person to knowingly use the mail service of the United States Postal Service or any interstate instrumentality for purposes of promoting or in any other manner furthering an animal fighting venture except as performed outside the limits of the States of the United States.

"(d) Not withstanding the provisions of subsection (a), (b), or © of this section, the activities prohibited by such subsection shall be unlawful with respect to fighting ventures involving live birds only if the fight is to take place in a State where it would be in violation of the laws thereof.

"(e) Any person who violates subsection (a), (b), or © shall be fined not more than $5,000 or imprisoned for not more than 1 year, or both, for each such violation.

[Investigation. Warrant. Costs, recovery.] "(f) The Secretary or any other person authorized by him shall make such investigations as the Secretary deems necessary to determine whether any person has violated or is violating any provision of this section, and the Secretary may obtain the assistance of the Federal Bureau of Investigation, the Department of the Treasury, or other law enforcement agencies of the United States, and State and local governmental agencies, in the conduct of such investigations, under cooperative agreements with such agencies. A warrant to search for and seize any animal which there is probable cause to believe was involved in any violation of this section may be issued by any judge of the United States or of a State court of record or by a United States magistrate within the district wherein the animal sought is located. Any United States marshal or any person authorized under this section to conduct investigations may apply for and execute any such warrant, and any animal seized under such a warrant shall be held by the United States marshal or other authorized person pending disposition thereof by the court in accordance with this paragraph (f). Necessary care including veterinary treatment shall be provided while the animals are so held in custody. Any animal involved in any violation of this section shall be liable to be proceeded against and forfeited to the United States at any time on complaint filed in any United States district court or other court of the United States for any jurisdiction in which the animal is found and upon a judgment of forfeiture shall be disposed of by sale for lawful purposes or by other humane means, as the court may direct. Costs incurred by the United States for care of animals seized and forfeited under this section shall be recoverable from the owner of the animals if he appears in such forfeiture proceeding or in a separate civil action brought in the jurisdiction in which the owner is found, resides, or transacts business.

[Definitions.] "(g) For purposes of this section--

"(1) the term `animal fighting venture' means any event which involves a fight between at least two animals and is conducted for purposes of sport, wagering, or entertainment except that the term for `animal fighting venture' shall not be deemed to include any activity the primary purpose of which involves the use of one or more animals in hunting another animal or animals, such as waterfowl, bird, raccoon, or fox hunting;

"(2) the term `interstate or foreign commerce' means--

"(A) any movement between any place in a State to any place in another State or between places in the same State through another State; or

"(B) any movement from a foreign country into any State;

"(3) the term `interstate instrumentality' means telegraph, telephone, radio, or television operating interstate or foreign commerce;

"(4) the term `State' means any State of the United States, the District of Columbia, the Commonwealth of Puerto Rico, and any territory or possession of the United States;

"(5) the term `animal' means any live bird, or any live dog or other mammal, except man; and

"(6) the conduct by any person of any activity prohibited by this section shall not render such person subject to the other sections of this Act as a dealer, exhibitor, or otherwise.

"(h)(1) The provisions of this Act shall not supersede or otherwise invalidate any such State, local, or municipal legislation or ordinance relating to animal fighting ventures except in case of a direct and irreconcilable conflict between any requirements there under and this Act or any rule, regulation, or standard hereunder.

[Ante, p. 421.] "(2) Section 3001(a) of title 39, United States Code, is amended by adding immediately after the words `title 18 ' a comma and the words `or section 26 of the Animal Welfare Act'."

[7 USC 2153.] SEC. 18. Section 23 of such Act is amended by inserting immediately before the period at the end of the third sentence "; Provided, That there is authorized to be appropriated to the Secretary of Agriculture for enforcement by the Department of Agriculture of the provisions of section 26 of this Act an amount not to exceed $100,000 for the transition quarter ending September 30, 1976, and not to exceed $400,000 for each fiscal year thereafter".

[7 USC 2144.] SEC. 19. Section 14 of such Act is amended by inserting in the first sentence after the term "standards" the phrase "and other requirements".

Isn't it amazing to read this Act? It's quite a lengthy document that has gone through revisions and additions over the years. What you may find also amazing and in no means is this advocacy for pro-choice or pro-life situations, is that an unborn child, "alive" (alive is a general term since we collectively as the United States cannot agree on when a fetus is actually a "baby") in the womb doesn't have the same protection. It would seem a typical housecat has more rights than a fetus. That's interesting.

Chapter 6

60 Days to Make a Winner

Through the previous chapters of this book, we have discussed the correct manner in which someone interested in dog fighting should conduct the sport. Now we're going to take a look at the proper way to condition your dog. This is a sure fire way to your dog is in top shape when it comes time to enter the ring. I call this no fail system: *Guillory's 60-Day Keep*.

Guillory's 60-Day PitBull Keep.

Day 1

* Hand walk for 2 miles and allow dog to relieve himself.

* Weigh dog and record his weight.

* Weight Pull with harness & tracers for 5 minutes at ¼ bodyweight.

* Flirt Pole for 5 minutes.

* Treadmill for 5 minutes.

* Spring pole for 5 minutes.

* Swim tank for 5 minutes.

* Walk dog at his pace for 2 miles to allow him to regain his normal breathing pattern but do not allow dog to sit at anytime during any part of his exercise routines or anytime between them when going from 1 routine to another.

* Give the dog his full body massage and talk to him.

Day 2

* Hand walk for 2 miles and allow dog to relieve himself.

* Weigh dog and record his weight.

* Weight Pull with harness & tracers for 5 minutes at ¼ bodyweight.

* Flirt Pole for 5 minutes.

* Treadmill for 5 minutes.

* Spring pole for 5 minutes.

* Swim tank for 5 minutes.

* Walk dog at his pace for 2 miles to allow him to regain his normal breathing pattern but do not allow dog to sit at anytime during any part of his exercise routines or anytime between them when going from 1 routine to another.

* Give the dog his full body massage and talk to him.

Day 3

* Hand walk for 2 miles and allow dog to relieve himself.

* Weight dog and record his weight.

* Give the dog his full body massage and talk to him.

Day 4

* Hand walk for 2 miles and allow dog to relieve himself.

* Weigh dog and record his weight.

* Weight Pull with harness & tracers for 5 minutes at ¼ bodyweight.

* Flirt Pole for 5 minutes.

* Treadmill for 5 minutes.

* Spring pole for 5 minutes.

* Swim tank for 5 minutes.

* Walk dog at his pace for 2 miles to allow him to regain his normal breathing pattern but do not allow dog to sit at anytime during any part of his exercise routines or anytime between them when going from 1 routine to another.

* Give the dog his full body massage and talk to him.

Day 5

* Hand walk for 2 miles and allow dog to relieve himself.

* Weigh dog and record his weight.

* Weight Pull with harness & tracers for 5 minutes at ¼ bodyweight.

* Flirt Pole for 5 minutes.

* Treadmill for 5 minutes.

* Spring pole for 5 minutes.

* Swim tank for 5 minutes.

* Walk dog at his pace for 2 miles to allow him to regain his normal breathing pattern but do not allow dog to sit at anytime during any part of his exercise routines or anytime between them when going from 1 routine to another.

* Give the dog his full body massage and talk to him.

Day 6

* Hand walk for 2 miles and allow dog to relieve himself.

* Weight dog and record his weight.

* Give the dog his full body massage and talk to him.

 Day 7

* Hand walk for 2 miles and allow dog to relieve himself.

* Weight dog and record his weight.

* Give the dog his full body massage and talk to him.

Day 8

* Hand walk for 2 miles and allow dog to relieve himself.

* Weigh dog and record his weight.

* Weight Pull with harness & tracers for 7 minutes at ¼ bodyweight.

* Flirt Pole for 7 minutes.

* Treadmill for 7 minutes.

* Spring pole for 7 minutes.

* Swim tank for 7 minutes.

* Walk dog at his pace for 2 miles to allow him to regain his normal breathing pattern but do not allow dog to sit at anytime during any part of his exercise routines or anytime between them when going from 1 routine to another.

* Give the dog his full body massage and talk to him.

Day 9

* Hand walk for 2 miles and allow dog to relieve himself.

* Weigh dog and record his weight.

* Weight Pull with harness & tracers for 7 minutes at ¼ bodyweight.

* Flirt Pole for 7 minutes.

* Treadmill for 7 minutes.

* Spring pole for 7 minutes.

* Swim tank for 7 minutes.

* Walk dog at his pace for 2 miles to allow him to regain his normal breathing pattern but do not allow dog to sit at anytime during any part of his exercise routines or anytime between them when going from 1 routine to another.

* Give the dog his full body massage and talk to him.

Day 10

* Hand walk for 2 miles and allow dog to relieve himself.

* Weight dog and record his weight.

* Give the dog his full body massage and talk to him.

Day 11

* Hand walk for 2 miles and allow dog to relieve himself.

* Weight dog and record his weight.

* Give the dog his full body massage and talk to him.

Day 12

* Hand walk for 2 miles and allow dog to relieve himself.

* Weigh dog and record his weight.

* Weight Pull with harness & tracers for 10 minutes at ¼ bodyweight.

* Flirt Pole for 10 minutes.

* Treadmill for 10 minutes.

* Spring pole for 10 minutes.

* Swim tank for 10 minutes.

* Walk dog at his pace for 2 miles to allow him to regain his normal breathing pattern but do not allow dog to sit at anytime during any part of his exercise routines or anytime between them when going from 1 routine to another.

* Give the dog his full body massage and talk to him.

Day 13

* Hand walk for 2 miles and allow dog to relieve himself.

* Weigh dog and record his weight.

* Weight Pull with harness & tracers for 10 minutes at ¼ bodyweight.

* Flirt Pole for 10 minutes.

* Treadmill for 10 minutes.

* Spring pole for 10 minutes.

* Swim tank for 10 minutes.

* Walk dog at his pace for 2 miles to allow him to regain his normal breathing pattern but do not allow dog to sit at anytime during any part of his exercise routines or anytime between them when going from 1 routine to another.

* Give the dog his full body massage and talk to him.

Day 14

* Hand walk for 2 miles and allow dog to relieve himself.

* Weight dog and record his weight.

* Give the dog his full body massage and talk to him.

Day 15

* Hand walk for 2 miles and allow dog to relieve himself.

* Weight dog and record his weight.

* Give the dog his full body massage and talk to him.

Day 16

* Hand walk for 2 miles and allow dog to relieve himself.

* Weigh dog and record his weight.

* Weight Pull with harness & tracers for 10 minutes at ¼ bodyweight.

* Flirt Pole for 15 minutes.

* Treadmill for 15 minutes.

* Spring pole for 15 minutes.

* Swim tank for 15 minutes.

* Walk dog at his pace for 2 miles to allow him to regain his normal breathing pattern but do not allow dog to sit at anytime during any part of his exercise routines or anytime between them when going from 1 routine to another.

* Give the dog his full body massage and talk to him.

Day 17

* Hand walk for 2 miles and allow dog to relieve himself.

* Weigh dog and record his weight.

* Weight Pull with harness & tracers for 10 minutes at ¼ bodyweight.

* Flirt Pole for 15 minutes.

* Treadmill for 15 minutes.

* Spring pole for 15 minutes.

* Swim tank for 15 minutes.

* Walk dog at his pace for 2 miles to allow him to regain his normal breathing pattern but do not allow dog to sit at anytime during any part of his exercise routines or anytime between them when going from 1 routine to another.

* Give the dog his full body massage and talk to him.

Day 18

* Hand walk for 2 miles and allow dog to relieve himself.

* Weight dog and record his weight.

* Give the dog his full body massage and talk to him.

Day 19

* Hand walk for 2 miles and allow dog to relieve himself.

* Weight dog and record his weight.

* Give the dog his full body massage and talk to him.

Day 20

* Hand walk for 2 miles and allow dog to relieve himself.

* Weigh dog and record his weight.

* Weight Pull with harness & tracers for 10 minutes at ¼ bodyweight.

* Flirt Pole for 15 minutes.

* Treadmill for 15 minutes.

* Spring pole for 15 minutes.

* Swim tank for 15 minutes.

* Walk dog at his pace for 2 miles to allow him to regain his normal breathing pattern but do not allow dog to sit at anytime during any part of his exercise routines or anytime between them when going from 1 routine to another.

* Give the dog his full body massage and talk to him.

Day 21

* Hand walk for 2 miles and allow dog to relieve himself.

* Weigh dog and record his weight.

* Weight Pull with harness & tracers for 10 minutes at ¼ bodyweight.

* Flirt Pole for 15 minutes.

* Treadmill for 15 minutes.

* Spring pole for 15 minutes.

* Swim tank for 15 minutes.

* Walk dog at his pace for 2 miles to allow him to regain his normal breathing pattern but do not allow dog to sit at anytime during any part of his exercise routines or anytime between them when going from 1 routine to another.

* Give the dog his full body massage and talk to him.

Day 22

* Hand walk for 2 miles and allow dog to relieve himself.

* Weight dog and record his weight.

* Give the dog his full body massage and talk to him.

Day 23

* Hand walk for 2 miles and allow dog to relieve himself.

* Weight dog and record his weight.

* Give the dog his full body massage and talk to him.

Day 24

* Hand walk for 2 miles and allow dog to relieve himself.

* Weigh dog and record his weight.

* Weight Pull with harness & tracers for 10 minutes at ¼ bodyweight.

* Flirt Pole for 15 minutes.

* Treadmill for 15 minutes.

* Spring pole for 15 minutes.

* Swim tank for 15 minutes.

* Walk dog at his pace for 2 miles to allow him to regain his normal breathing pattern but do not allow dog to sit at anytime during any part of his exercise routines or anytime between them when going from 1 routine to another.

* Give the dog his full body massage and talk to him.

Day 25

* Hand walk for 2 miles and allow dog to relieve himself.

* Weigh dog and record his weight.

* Weight Pull with harness & tracers for 10 minutes at ¼ bodyweight.

* Flirt Pole for 15 minutes.

* Treadmill for 15 minutes.

* Spring pole for 15 minutes.

* Swim tank for 15 minutes.

* Walk dog at his pace for 2 miles to allow him to regain his normal breathing pattern but do not allow dog to sit at anytime during any part of his exercise routines or anytime between them when going from 1 routine to another.

* Give the dog his full body massage and talk to him.

Day 26

* Hand walk for 2 miles and allow dog to relieve himself.

* Weight dog and record his weight.

* Give the dog his full body massage and talk to him.

Day 27

* Hand walk for 2 miles and allow dog to relieve himself.

* Weight dog and record his weight.

* Give the dog his full body massage and talk to him.

Day 28

* Hand walk for 2 miles and allow dog to relieve himself.

* Weigh dog and record his weight.

* Weight Pull with harness & tracers for 10 minutes at ¼ bodyweight.

* Flirt Pole for 15 minutes.

* Treadmill for 15 minutes.

* Spring pole for 15 minutes.

* Swim tank for 15 minutes.

* Walk dog at his pace for 2 miles to allow him to regain his normal breathing pattern but do not allow dog to sit at anytime during any part of his exercise routines or anytime between them when going from 1 routine to another.

* Give the dog his full body massage and talk to him.

Day 29

* Hand walk for 2 miles and allow dog to relieve himself.

* Weigh dog and record his weight.

* Weight Pull with harness & tracers for 10 minutes at ¼ bodyweight.

* Flirt Pole for 15 minutes.

* Treadmill for 15 minutes.

* Spring pole for 15 minutes.

* Swim tank for 15 minutes.

* Walk dog at his pace for 2 miles to allow him to regain his normal breathing pattern but do not allow dog to sit at anytime during any part of his exercise routines or anytime between them when going from 1 routine to another.

* Give the dog his full body massage and talk to him.

Day 30

* Hand walk for 2 miles and allow dog to relieve himself.

* Weigh dog and record his weight.

* Weight Pull with harness & tracers for 10 minutes at ¼ bodyweight.

* Flirt Pole for 15 minutes.

* Treadmill for 15 minutes.

* Spring pole for 15 minutes.

* Swim tank for 15 minutes.

* Walk dog at his pace for 2 miles to allow him to regain his normal breathing pattern but do not allow dog to sit at anytime during any part of his exercise routines or anytime between them when going from 1 routine to another.

* Give the dog his full body massage and talk to him.

Day 31

* Hand walk for 2 miles and allow dog to relieve himself.

* Weight dog and record his weight.

* Give the dog his full body massage and talk to him.

Day 32

* Hand walk for 2 miles and allow dog to relieve himself.

* Weigh dog and record his weight.

* Weight Pull with harness & tracers for 17 minutes at ½ bodyweight.

* Flirt Pole for 17 minutes.

* Treadmill for 17 minutes.

* Spring pole for 17 minutes.

* Swim tank for 17 minutes.

* Walk dog at his pace for 2 miles to allow him to regain his normal breathing pattern but do not allow dog to sit at anytime during any part of his exercise routines or anytime between them when going from 1 routine to another.

* Give the dog his full body massage and talk to him.

Day 33

* Hand walk for 2 miles and allow dog to relieve himself.

* Weigh dog and record his weight.

* Weight Pull with harness & tracers for 17 minutes at ½ bodyweight.

* Flirt Pole for 17 minutes.

* Treadmill for 17 minutes.

* Spring pole for 17 minutes.

* Swim tank for 17 minutes.

* Walk dog at his pace for 2 miles to allow him to regain his normal breathing pattern but do not allow dog to sit at anytime during any part of his exercise routines or anytime between them when going from 1 routine to another.

* Give the dog his full body massage and talk to him.

Day 34

* Hand walk for 2 miles and allow dog to relieve himself.

* Weigh dog and record his weight.

* Weight Pull with harness & tracers for 17 minutes at ½ bodyweight.

* Flirt Pole for 17 minutes.

* Treadmill for 17 minutes.

* Spring pole for 17 minutes.

* Swim tank for 17 minutes.

* Walk dog at his pace for 2 miles to allow him to regain his normal breathing pattern but do not allow dog to sit at anytime during any part of his exercise routines or anytime between them when going from 1 routine to another.

* Give the dog his full body massage and talk to him.

Day 35

* Hand walk for 2 miles and allow dog to relieve himself.

* Weight dog and record his weight.

* Give the dog his full body massage and talk to him.

Day 36

* Hand walk for 2 miles and allow dog to relieve himself.

* Weight dog and record his weight.

* Give the dog his full body massage and talk to him.

Day 37

* Hand walk for 2 miles and allow dog to relieve himself.

* Weight dog and record his weight.

* Give the dog his full body massage and talk to him.

Day 38

* Hand walk for 2 miles and allow dog to relieve himself.

* Weigh dog and record his weight.

* Weight Pull with harness & tracers for 20 minutes at ½ bodyweight.

* Flirt Pole for 20 minutes.

* Treadmill for 20 minutes.

* Spring pole for 20 minutes.

* Swim tank for 20 minutes.

* Walk dog at his pace for 2 miles to allow him to regain his normal breathing pattern but do not allow dog to sit at anytime during any part of his exercise routines or anytime between them when going from 1 routine to another.

* Give the dog his full body massage and talk to him.

Day 39

* Hand walk for 2 miles and allow dog to relieve himself.

* Weigh dog and record his weight.

* Weight Pull with harness & tracers for 20 minutes at ½ bodyweight.

* Flirt Pole for 20 minutes.

* Treadmill for 20 minutes.

* Spring pole for 20 minutes.

* Swim tank for 20 minutes.

* Walk dog at his pace for 2 miles to allow him to regain his normal breathing pattern but do not allow dog to sit at anytime during any part of his exercise routines or anytime between them when going from 1 routine to another.

* Give the dog his full body massage and talk to him.

Day 40

* Hand walk for 2 miles and allow dog to relieve himself.

* Weigh dog and record his weight.

* Weight Pull with harness & tracers for 20 minutes at ½ bodyweight.

* Flirt Pole for 20 minutes.

* Treadmill for 20 minutes.

* Spring pole for 20 minutes.

* Swim tank for 20 minutes.

* Walk dog at his pace for 2 miles to allow him to regain his normal breathing pattern but do not allow dog to sit at anytime during any part of his exercise routines or anytime between them when going from 1 routine to another.

* Give the dog his full body massage and talk to him.

Day 41

* Hand walk for 2 miles and allow dog to relieve himself.

* Weight dog and record his weight.

* Give the dog his full body massage and talk to him.

Day 42

* Hand walk for 2 miles and allow dog to relieve himself.

* Weight dog and record his weight.

* Give the dog his full body massage and talk to him.

Day 43

* Hand walk for 2 miles and allow dog to relieve himself.

* Weight dog and record his weight.

* Give the dog his full body massage and talk to him.

Day 44

* Hand walk for 2 miles and allow dog to relieve himself.

* Weigh dog and record his weight.

* Weight Pull with harness & tracers for 30 minutes at ¾ bodyweight.

* Flirt Pole for 30 minutes.

* Treadmill for 30 minutes.

* Spring pole for 30 minutes.

* Swim tank for 30 minutes.

* Walk dog at his pace for 2 miles to allow him to regain his normal breathing pattern but do not allow dog to sit at anytime during any part of his exercise routines or anytime between them when going from 1 routine to another.

* Give the dog his full body massage and talk to him.

Day 45

* Hand walk for 2 miles and allow dog to relieve himself.

* Weigh dog and record his weight.

* Weight Pull with harness & tracers for 30 minutes at ¾ bodyweight.

* Flirt Pole for 30 minutes.

* Treadmill for 30 minutes.

* Spring pole for 30 minutes.

* Swim tank for 30 minutes.

* Walk dog at his pace for 2 miles to allow him to regain his normal breathing pattern but do not allow dog to sit at anytime during any part of his exercise routines or anytime between them when going from 1 routine to another.

* Give the dog his full body massage and talk to him.

Day 46

* Hand walk for 2 miles and allow dog to relieve himself.

* Weigh dog and record his weight.

* Weight Pull with harness & tracers for 30 minutes at ¾ bodyweight.

* Flirt Pole for 30 minutes.

* Treadmill for 30 minutes.

* Spring pole for 30 minutes.

* Swim tank for 30 minutes.

* Walk dog at his pace for 2 miles to allow him to regain his normal breathing pattern but do not allow dog to sit at anytime during any part of his exercise routines or anytime between them when going from 1 routine to another.

* Give the dog his full body massage and talk to him.

Day 47

* Hand walk for 2 miles and allow dog to relieve himself.

* Weight dog and record his weight.

* Give the dog his full body massage and talk to him.

Day 48

* Hand walk for 2 miles and allow dog to relieve himself.

* Weight dog and record his weight.

* Give the dog his full body massage and talk to him.

Day 49

* Hand walk for 2 miles and allow dog to relieve himself.

* Weigh dog and record his weight.

* Weight Pull with harness & tracers for 30 minutes at ¾ bodyweight.

* Flirt Pole for 30 minutes.

* Treadmill for 30 minutes.

* Spring pole for 30 minutes.

* Swim tank for 30 minutes.

* Walk dog at his pace for 2 miles to allow him to regain his normal breathing pattern but do not allow dog to sit at anytime during any part of his exercise routines or anytime between them when going from 1 routine to another.

* Give the dog his full body massage and talk to him.

 Day 50

* Hand walk for 2 miles and allow dog to relieve himself.

* Weigh dog and record his weight.

* Weight Pull with harness & tracers for 30 minutes at ¾ bodyweight.

* Flirt Pole for 30 minutes.

* Treadmill for 30 minutes.

* Spring pole for 30 minutes.

* Swim tank for 30 minutes.

* Walk dog at his pace for 2 miles to allow him to regain his normal breathing pattern but do not allow dog to sit at anytime during any part of his exercise routines or anytime between them when going from 1 routine to another.

* Give the dog his full body massage and talk to him.

Day 51

* Hand walk for 2 miles and allow dog to relieve himself.

* Weigh dog and record his weight.

* Weight Pull with harness & tracers for 30 minutes at ¾ bodyweight.

* Flirt Pole for 30 minutes.

* Treadmill for 30 minutes.

* Spring pole for 30 minutes.

* Swim tank for 30 minutes.

* Walk dog at his pace for 2 miles to allow him to regain his normal breathing pattern but do not allow dog to sit at anytime during any part of his exercise routines or anytime between them when going from 1 routine to another.

* Give the dog his full body massage and talk to him.

Day 52

* Hand walk for 2 miles and allow dog to relieve himself.

* Weight dog and record his weight.

* Give the dog his full body massage and talk to him.

Day 53

* Hand walk for 2 miles and allow dog to relieve himself.

* Weight dog and record his weight.

* Give the dog his full body massage and talk to him.

Day 54

* Hand walk for 2 miles and allow dog to relieve himself.

* Weigh dog and record his weight.

* Weight Pull with harness & tracers for 15 minutes at ¼ bodyweight.

* Flirt Pole for 15 minutes.

* Treadmill for 15 minutes.

* Spring pole for 15 minutes.

* Swim tank for 15 minutes.

* Walk dog at his pace for 2 miles to allow him to regain his normal breathing pattern but do not allow dog to sit at anytime during any part of his exercise routines or anytime between them when going from 1 routine to another.

* Give the dog his full body massage and talk to him.

Day 55

* Hand walk for 2 miles and allow dog to relieve himself.

* Weigh dog and record his weight.

* Weight Pull with harness & tracers for 15 minutes at ¼ bodyweight.

* Flirt Pole for 15 minutes.

* Treadmill for 15 minutes.

* Spring pole for 15 minutes.

* Swim tank for 15 minutes.

* Walk dog at his pace for 2 miles to allow him to regain his normal breathing pattern but do not allow dog to sit at anytime during any part of his exercise routines or anytime between them when going from 1 routine to another.

* Give the dog his full body massage and talk to him.

Day 56

* Hand walk for 2 miles and allow dog to relieve himself.

* Weigh dog and record his weight.

* Treadmill for 15 minutes.

* Swim tank for 15 minutes.

* Walk dog at his pace for 2 miles to allow him to regain his normal breathing pattern but do not allow dog to sit at anytime during any part of his exercise routines or anytime between them when going from 1 routine to another.

* Give the dog his full body massage and talk to him.

Day 57

* Hand walk for 2 miles and allow dog to relieve himself.

* Weigh dog and record his weight.

* Treadmill for 5 minutes.

* Swim tank for 5 minutes.

* Walk dog at his pace for 2 miles to allow him to regain his normal breathing pattern but do not allow dog to sit at anytime during any part of his exercise routines or anytime between them when going from 1 routine to another.

* Give the dog his full body massage and talk to him.

Day 58

* Hand walk for 1 mile and allow dog to relieve himself.

* Weight dog and record his weight.

* Give the dog his full body massage and talk to him.

Day 59

* Hand walk for 1 mile and allow dog to relieve himself.

* Weight dog and record his weight.

* Give the dog his full body massage and talk to him.

Day 60

SHOWTIME.

By now your dog should be at his best physical condition, and therefore, ready to take on his opponents. Exercise is an important factor in the health and power of your animal, but that isn't all. The next chapter will take you through a proper diet regimen your dog should follow. But before we look at diets, let's take a look at a similar training regime, only this time it's a 14-day course tailored to get your gamecock in top shape.

Guillory's 14 Day Gamecock Keep

Day 1

20 Jumps.

20 Runs.

Hanging fly till completion.

Pull down fly till completion.

Vigorously rub roosters back.

Throat rub.

Massage legs with rubbing alcohol.

Day 2

40 Jumps.

40 Runs.

Hanging fly till completion.

Pull down fly till completion.

Vigorously rub roosters back.

Throat rub.

Massage legs with rubbing alcohol.

Day 3

60 Jumps.

60 Runs.

Hanging fly till completion.

Pull down fly till completion.

Vigorously rub roosters back.

Throat rub.

Massage legs with rubbing alcohol.

Day 4

80 Jumps.

80 Runs.

Hanging fly till completion.

Pull down fly till completion.

Vigorously rub roosters back.

Throat rub.

Massage legs with rubbing alcohol

Day 5

100 Jumps.

100 Runs.

Hanging fly till completion.

Pull down fly till completion.

Vigorously rub roosters back.

Throat rub.

Massage legs with rubbing alcohol.

Day 6

120 Jumps.

120 Runs.

Hanging fly till completion.

Pull down fly till completion.

Vigorously rub roosters back.

Throat rub.

Massage legs with rubbing alcohol.

Day 7

140 Jumps.

140 Runs.

Hanging fly till completion.

Pull down fly till completion.

Vigorously rub roosters back.

Throat rub.

Massage legs with rubbing alcohol

Day 8

160 Jumps.

160 Runs.

Hanging fly till completion.

Pull down fly till completion.

Vigorously rub roosters back.

Throat rub.

Massage legs with rubbing alcohol.

Day 9

160 Jumps.

160 Runs.

Hanging fly till completion.

Pull down fly till completion.

Vigorously rub roosters back.

Throat rub.

Massage legs with rubbing alcohol.

Day 10

140 Jumps.

140 Runs.

Hanging fly till completion.

Pull down fly till completion.

Vigorously rub roosters back.

Throat rub.

Massage legs with rubbing alcohol.

Day 11

120 Jumps.

120 Runs.

Hanging fly till completion.

Pull down fly till completion.

Vigorously rub roosters back.

Throat rub.

Massage legs with rubbing alcohol.

Day 12

100 Jumps.

100 Runs.

Hanging fly till completion.

Pull down fly till completion.

Vigorously rub roosters back.

Throat rub.

Massage legs with rubbing alcohol.

Day 13

<u>NO WORK DONE.</u>

Vigorously rub roosters back.

Throat rub.

Massage legs with rubbing alcohol.

Only 2 sips of water.

Day 14 (Fight Day)

<u>NO WORK DONE.</u>

Vigorously rub roosters back.

Throat rub.

Massage legs with rubbing alcohol.

Normal feed amount in morning.

Only 2 sips of water.

Also, below are the definitions of the exercises mentioned above for both gamecocks:

Jump – Place 1 hand on back and 1 on chest. Pick up the bird a few inches and use the hand on the chest to push the gamecock backwards while pushing with the hand on the back. Allow the bird to land on its feet and back in position. *Do this as fast as the bird can do it, remember, the bird must be allowed to land on its feet. This builds up the bird's balance and wing power. To an extent it's endurance.*

Run – Hold the gamecock on the back and push him from one end of the table to the other and back again. This is one complete run. *The gamecock will have trouble at first but he will soon learn how to adjust to this.*

Hanging Fly – Hold the gamecock by the tail feathers, holding about halfway up the tail and grasp the area completely around with your hand and hold him just high enough so when he flaps his wings, his wing tips barely touch the table and allow him to do this until he no longer flaps his wings. *This will build his wing power and will increase his endurance enormously.*

Pull Down Fly – Place the gamecock near the edge of the table and hold by the tail feathers, holding about halfway up the tail and grasp the area completely around with hand and pull down just enough so the rooster will think he will fall off the table if he doesn't flap his wings and allow him to do this until he is almost completely devoid of any energy at this point. *This will build his wing power and will increase his endurance enormously.*

Chapter 7
Proper Dieting:
What You Need to Feed Your Dogs and Gamecocks

When it comes to training a lean, mean, fighting machine, a can of wet dog food simply will not do. Use this reference sheet and the one listed below as a guide to understanding proper feeding of your game animals. This is going to build their muscles, give them daily nutrition and make them essentially a well-oiled machine. Starving your dog isn't the way to win a fight. You need carbohydrates before you work out and animals aren't much different. Refer to the lists below.

Feeding Reference for Gamecocks

The Pre-Keep Feed

4 Cup Pigeon conditioning feed w/o corn

2-Cups Popcorn

½ Cup Sunflower Seed Hearts

Conditioning Feed

¼ Cup Pre-Keep Feed

1 Raw Egg, shells crushed and added

1 Tablespoon of chopped raw beef liver

1 Eye Dropper of Cold Water Alaskan Salmon Fish Oil

Feeding Reference for Dogs

Morning Meal

Vertex (4 tablespoons per 20 lb dog) 1 cup of purified water

1 Pill of Alaskan Cold Water Salmon Oil, 1,000mg per pill

1 Coenzyme Q-10, 60mg

Evening Meal to be given 1 hour after workouts

1 pound of ground chicken

Gluacosamine / Chondroitin, 750/600 mg.

Wheat Germ Oil, 1 ½ Tablespoon

2 cups of Greens Mixture, Greens Mixture is made up as follows:

1 part Shredded Collard Greens

1 part Shredded Baby Spinach

1 part Shredded Mustard Greens

1 part Turnip Greens

Take all parts and blend together and hand mix into the 1 pound of ground chicken and other ingredients.

Chapter 8
Stories from the Author

I'd like to share two stories with you. These stories are the actual accounts of my first experience with dog fighting and cock fighting. These narratives were the beginning for me. They fueled my passion for the sport, and kept it alive inside of me through the years.

My first dogfight was in Richard Louisiana on private property, in a barn located down an old gravel road back in the woods. There was an off duty state trooper that was directing traffic where to park, and another was checking to make sure all in attendance were not armed with any knives or guns. Safety for the animals and the attendants has always been a priority of mine.

The price for admission was $50.00 per person. We were led into the barn where there was a temporary pit set up, it was 16' x 16' x 2' high. It was a small gathering; I would estimate it to have less than 100 people.

The dogs were brought in and weighed; each one weighed 37 pounds exactly. In one corner was a black dog with only a small white star on its chest, and the other dog was a red brindle, or what some like to call "tiger stripe". The dogs were washed by the opposing handlers and were then brought to their corners.

After the normal preliminaries completed, the dogs were released and they charged into each other with every ounce of strength they had. You would think that being at a dog fight, you would hear a lot of barking and growling but it was eerily quiet. The dogs were wrestling to get a good hold on each other and were standing up on their hind legs with their heads trying to push the other's head out of the way to get a good bite. The black dog got its first hold and had the brindle dog by his ear, then used his leverage to bring the dog down on all fours. The black dog quickly released his bite and dropped his head and got his next bite square on the brindle's chest and went to work on it. The brindle was pushed backwards and fell over, but quickly grabbed the black's front left leg and held and shook for what seemed a really long time.

I noticed that both dogs had their tails either straight up or wagging. I asked my friend about it and he said that it was because they loved what they were doing. After awhile, a handler was called and both came in and used breaking sticks to separate the dogs so they could be brought to their prospective corners.
I watched as the dogs had water splashed in their mouths. Then a handful of water was held against their lower stomach. The dogs were turned to face each other and released. The black dog was released first and he came in charging hard and when the brindle was released, he immediately went under the black one and came behind and grabbed the black dog by the front left shoulder. They seemed as if they were bonded together by glue.

The brindle had the black's leg lifted slightly and held onto the shoulder as he pushed and pulled the black all over the pit. The black dog kept trying to break free, but every time he tried to break free, the brindle would twist his head towards his left into the black, which would put even more pressure on the black's shoulder.

I didn't notice the other people for a while because I was so amazed at the dogs, but after a few minutes I looked around and they were laughing and joking about the dogs. It wasn't as bad as when the fight began, but it surprised me to see others acting that way. It certainly wasn't how I felt watching these warriors.

The longer the fight went on, the quieter everyone became. Even the handlers were sitting on the walls of the pit, staring at the dogs. The brindle kept doing what he was doing for what seemed a very long time when the black finally broke loose and pushed hard under the brindle. He grabbed the brindle's chest and drove the brindle into the wall so hard that many thought the wooden wall had cracked! "Wow, what power!" I thought to myself.

The black and the brindle dogs were what are today considered to be "butter mouths." This means they couldn't chew butter with mouths that soft. These two dogs fought for over two hours, and it came down to which dog was the gamest dog. The brindle was eventually named the winner strictly because he had a better condition.

The referee was the first to say that they may have been soft mouths, but they were indeed game dogs! There was no mistake about that. They never quit, and as long as they had the strength, they crossed the line with determination. They loved what they were doing and they did it well.

There was an old timer there from Arizona. The brindle was actually born on his property. Many were going on an on about the "soft mouths" of these dogs, but it was about being a game dog…. not a hard mouth. The old man from Arizona said that he noticed that too many of the younger guys only thought about the quick money, instead of doing right by the tradition of breeding game dogs. He also noticed that they bred dogs that were considered to be man biters. Arizona, as I nick named him in my own mind, was talking with a man from my neck of the woods next to me, and he said that the younger guys would cause the end of the sport as they knew it because they didn't really care about the dogs. They only thought about the money. Some were breeding dogs that were not proven, hell they weren't even trying!

These younger guys only bred dogs to have a big yard so they could try to act as though they were some of the big boys. Their neighbors would think that because they had so many dogs, that they must be some of the best dogs and best dog men in the state. How else could they afford to feed so many dogs? They both laughed at that and walked away, talking something about some convention in a few weeks in Mississippi.

It wasn't very long afterwards that I got my first pit bull. I got him from Mr. J.K. in Church Point, Louisiana. J.K. was considered by many to be nothing more than a puppy peddler, but to be honest I got what I asked and paid for. I asked for a dog that had a bloodline that had proven itself. I got one that had amazing names four and five generations back, but were unproven up close.

I conditioned my dog and set up an off the chain "OTC" match to try him out against a good friend of mine that also fell in love with the dogs at the same time as myself. Our dogs went at it for 45 minutes until we stopped them. We were pleased with our dogs and our condition. My friend and I talked and in our "expert" opinion, our dogs could whip just about any dog out there. Now, I laugh at our inflated egos, but we really thought we had the best dogs in the country. We quickly found out how wrong we were! I won't bore anyone with the story. But let it be known, we grew up quick after that.

My first cockfight was in 1984. I was 15 years old and most of my friends were into rooster fights. As a teenage boy, naturally I wanted to fit in with my friends.

After long talks with my dad, he allowed me to go with a friend of the family who was also into the sport. We went to Matte's Rooster Pit in Church Point, Louisiana.

It was a cold Friday night in December. Admission was $2.00 so I paid and went straight to the benches, ring side seat. I sat down and atched as two men stepped into the pit with a rooster. a judge also entered the pit. The judge grabbed a lemon and stuck the lemon all the way onto each rooster's aluminum spur that was taped on each leg. The purpose was to draw any poisons that may have been put onto the spurs. It seemed that the sport had its unsavory characters, much like all sports.

The two men who held the roosters in the pit (called handlers or pitters) each took a corner across from each other. On the judge's word they released the birds and the birds ran towards each other, then stopped inches away. Their neck feathers were opened up to make themselves seem much bigger to the other gamecock, but neither seemed to worry too much. They watched, and would ever so slightly act as though they were about ready to throw the first strike, but they were just testing each other.

I was seated next to an old man named Mr. David Lejuene. He was in his 80's, and he grew up around cockfights. He got his start from his dad and he was very well respected in and around the sport. He asked me who my dad was and after I told him, he said he figured as much, because I look like my dad. Turns out he lived just a mile away from my home. He asked me if it was my first cockfight and I said "yes".

He then started to tell me that the roosters were testing each other to try to figure out how to throw the first strike. After the first two or three strikes were thrown, they would settle down and get to business. It took less than a minute for them to start getting to it, and they would trade strikes back and forth. Mr. David Lejuene asked me which one I thought was the better cutter and I was honest. I said, "I have no idea" because they were so fast that I couldn't see a damned thing. He laughed and said to stare between the roosters, to look at the ground on the other side right between the roosters themselves and I would notice something.

I did as he instructed and then I noticed something.

It seemed as though when I wasn't concentrating on each rooster, but instead looking just past the roosters that I could see every strike being thrown. I could see where they were actually hitting and if they were hitting at all! He then told me that neither one were worth a dime and I should wait to see the next fight because he knew the roosters, and knew it would be a good fight.

It took about 20 minutes for the current fight to finish, and I saw the next roosters coming into the pit. I recognized one to be a Red Cuban. Each began crowing before they entered the pit, showing desire to be let loose. The handlers set them free, and they met at the middle of the pit in a flurry of punches, I later learned that they were shuffling, which means they were throwing many strikes in a short time. A shuffle is actually like a hook punch thrown by a boxer and not many gamecocks possess the ability to shuffle correctly. It was interesting to watch.

These two gamecocks went at it full steam for about 10 minutes when the Redwing stuck his spur all the way into the other bird's (a Red) neck and couldn't get it out on his own. A handler was called. The pitters brought the roosters to their corners and looked them over, then on the count dropped them again. This time the Red came in fast and acted like he wanted to jump up and strike, but instead he dropped down and let the Redwing jump up and the Redwing knew he messed up as the Red came up from underneath and shredded the Redwing before it had a chance to land and regroup.

The Redwing took a lot of punishment but kept coming, but the Red also kept coming and then the Red dropped the Redwing with a straight shot to the ear. The Redwing didn't move; it was stone cold dead. The pitters shook hands and declared it a fair fight. I went home after watching close to 150 fights that Night, and only seven ended in fatality.

These were truly game birds, and they fought as long as their bodies let them. I fell in love with the sport after that night, and after a few weeks of begging my dad I got my first gamecock. It seemed as soon as I got my first one there were a few old timers that showed up at the house and asked my dad if they could help me get started. They dropped off cages of roosters and hens with the papers of the pedigree written on old pieces of papers. I was instructed by the best of the best in the ways of breeding, raising, feeding, conditioning, pitting and basic veterinary care of the birds.

I soon became much respected among the young and old alike and I was only 15 years old! The first rooster I conditioned was a three year old one-eyed rooster with a messed up beak. He had fought a year earlier and won but was hurt pretty bad. I got him free and put him in a battle royal. The battle royal is just like in wrestling. It could be three or more roosters in the pit at one time, and the last one standing wins.

The entry fee was $10.00 and there ended up being a total of 10 roosters in the pit. My rooster either killed or ran off every single rooster in there, and begged for more! I was so proud! The old timers came up to me, smiled and shook my hand and told me how proud they were of the way I took care of that rooster. I walked away with $100.00 and like my rooster, ready for more!

To make a really long story short, my father and I fought on average about 30 birds per year and had the best winning percentage for six years in a row. For two of those years we had a 90% win ratio. I would also say that during those years we did not fight Cuban style, we fought until a winner was declared. Cuban style has a time limit, and if neither bird kills or runs off the other bird, a draw is declared. I have heard many cock fighters claim not to have lost a fight in three years, but when I asked how many did they win, they get angry and raise their voice: I TOLD YOU I DIDN"T LOSE A FIGHT IN 3 YEARS!!!

I worry about the new guys coming into the sports of cock fighting and dog fighting. They read a book and pay for a big name bloodline and think they are among the best. They're in it for the money. They have no appreciation for the sport; they just want to get paid. God save our sport.

Meet the Author:
Mr. Anthony Troy Guillory

Troy Guillory was born in Church Point Louisiana, just five miles away from the small farming community of Richard.

The Church Point/Richard area is arguably the center of Cajun culture. The area has more professional Cajun musicians than any other area in Louisiana. Mr. Guillory feels truly blessed to be brought up in such a richly cultured part of the United States.

It is also an area where there is an abundance of truly professional cock fighters, which is still legal in the state of Louisiana for the time being. The area is also home to some dog fighters, but in all honestly, the majority of the handlers are not so professional.

Mr. Guillory did not come from a family of cock fighters or dog fighters, but since he grew up in the area, he soon fell in love first with the sport of cock fighting and was blessed to have the access to some of the best
game fowl and some of the best coinciding advice.
Troy became very successful in both breeding and fighting
game fowl.

Mr. Guillory became interested in American Pit bull terriers because of their natural beauty, confidence and strength. The sport he first became interested with that involved the breed was weight pulling, but he is no stranger to the ring. He has been a spectator for many dogfights. He will continue to fight to defend the sport he is so passionate about.

Fire Girl. Photos cannot be copied or used in any way without the consent of the author.

The End.